CHANTERELLES

CHANTERELLES

Poems

Hal Steven Shows

Redhawk Publications
The Catawba Valley Community College Press
2550 US Hwy 70 SE
Hickory NC 28602

ISBN: 978-1-959346-15-9

Library of Congress Number: 2023942954

Printed in the United States of America

redhawkpublications.com

Layout and Cover By: Jim Lōser

This is dedicated to the one I love –

Contents

A Letter from the Occupation

Purely for purposes of pacification
we are clearing away the enemy's past.
When our officers gesture
across the river to the tiled roofs
and the hushed cortiles where the cypress rise
their gloved hands are indicating
new highways, necessary eliminations . . .

My job is mining the bridges.
Today, as I packed the plastic bombs
and fastened fine wire fuse
to the rough stone of the old foundation,
knee-deep in a heavy current,
something like sleep, a sudden trance
of memory and remorse ravished me.

I came to stock-still in the shallows,
close to the occupied bank.
Through gathering dusk I could see
desolate doors of deserted houses swaying ajar.
Betrayed, betraying, I had almost gone over
To an erstwhile enemy—a phantom—
though nothing is left in our wake.

American Dream

It's more like
wandering through a theme park
with no theme . . .

Analysis

I dreamed of you
And your eyes were the sightless
stone of ancient statues—
But It was myself I saw,
Still unawakened,
Brought before the law . . .

At the Station

The train was 2 hours late.
There was no one around,
no one in the station.
Suddenly the pay phone started
ringing at the other end of the platform.
I picked up my one heavy suitcase,
trudged down there,
and picked up the phone.
It was Amtrak informing me
that my train was 3 hours late.
For a brief glorious moment,
I felt like Buster Keaton.

Azaleas

yellow butterflies
dancing in our azaleas—
chimes of morning light!

Barroom

I love the clamor
of a barroom,
where everything
is equally urgent
and meaningless.

Bears

I hear that the killing
of as many as 327 bears
will not significantly harm
Florida's bear population—
individual bears
may take it hard, though.

Belief

I don't *believe* in anything,
In that sense,
Do you?

Aside from the sun, the moon—
The sky and the weather—
In this we are all together.

All the rest is whim,
And vanity, and cruelty . . .
And a fever of old.

Birds

I can calmly forsee a world
  without people,
Silent, the Earth slowly licking its
  luminous wounds—
But It's sad beyond sight and sound
To imagine a world without birds.

Blue

I love that blue look
late in the day
as shadows fall on the snow.

Branding

They can't classify
What they don't understand;

If they can't classify it
They have to deny it.

And once it escapes
Every classification

It is roundly decried
As a threat to the nation

When at best it was less
Than a passing sensation.

Brother Robert

My brother Robert killed his brother.
It happened fast and turned them both to stone.
It might have been I; I might have been another.

The winter was white and rigid as a bone
Left weathering unseen in distant sand.
At the last moment of course I am alone.

The live wire lashed the sodden land.
Around the boy a haze of cobalt rose.
In the end there was nothing to understand.

They gave me a hat and a suit of clothes
And pierced my skin with fabulous bits of bling.
How I survived my schooling Heaven knows.

Now, from scene to scene I swing,
Netless in the dark, with a foolish grin—
Whatever I need to say I try to sing

In unison with whatever band I'm in,
Like a lurid siren looking for a lover,
In the tightening circle of a single fin.

By Dark

We knew we were meant
To be in by dark—
But they couldn't find us;
We politely declined.
The rules defined the frontier
And everything strange
Was over there, where the sun set,
On the other side.

Cassandra

I told you before:
When it was done the drowsy god rolled over.
His heavy arm pinned my shoulders to the sand
As the risen moon burned the shadow of a breached wall
Across the beach.

At last a dark, winged dream descended.
Long before dawn, over the murmur of motherless children,
Men who were horses barking orders in a barbarous tongue
Herded us into Hell.

Cell to Cell

Bailey was stuck on his
Cellular phone
Fully connected but all alone
Wearing his striped pajamas
Talking to Christopher
Mallory-Horne
Who was living it up
In a tropical storm
In a bank in the Bahamas
Old Bailey said Chris
There is something amiss
In the heart of the USA
Mallory-Horne
To the manor born
With his stiff upper lip
In a sneer of scorn said
How can you live that way?

Citadel

I dreamed of a distant
Citadel, all unknown,
Approachable only
By ancient causeways
Over unholy seas.

Covent Garden

There, in the back booth
Of a shabby pub,
I happened upon a small
But well-burnished
Bronze plaque that read:
"Here the great
Poet John Dryden
Took his daily libations,"
And so to himself
I raised an imperial pint.

Covid 1

"I am a realist— If I get it, I get it!"
That's not realism—
That's mysticism;
That's magical thinking.

Covid 2

"If God wants me to get Covid, I will;
if he doesn't, I won't.
It is all in his hands."
When I was back in Sunday School,
They always told me
"God helps those who help themselves."

Death

Death affords us few liberties
As far as we know—

And each resists in strangled terror
When it's time to go—

Yet none return to say
"I told you so!"

Discipline

Love lights the way

Devotion is
Doing it every day

Discipline is
Doing it anyway

Doomsday

The men and women lay abed,
The mimes were laughing silently,
The frowning clowns concealed their faces.
And all the animals gathered round
The funeral of the human races.

The kisses that could not be stolen
Faded in the setting sun.
Murderous ideologies
Competed with mythologies
For kingdoms that could not be won.

The televisions testified
That none had told the truth, nor lied;
At last the businessmen went blind.
And then the angels sang aloud
An orizon for humankind.

So doomsday came—but no one knew,
For nothing was the least surprising—
The children's final prayers were said,
The men and women lay abed—
But all was changed, and tides were rising.

Eagle

It is not the fault
Of the Eagle
That Nazis
Polluted his nest.

Eau Gallie

It was my first Library.
I can feel the summer heat
On my neck and shoulders
As I take the broken sidewalk through
The gassy traffic under the sudden shade
Of the oaks toward the white building
Where the books are.

Eggshells

Whenever
You enter
the room I feel
I am sitting
on devilish eggshells
and my gall
starts to rise

Elvis in Jacksonville

The Jacksonville Police
Filmed the entire show
So prosecutors could determine
Whether The King had committed
Any obscene or suggestive
Gyrations that might imperil
The honor of the demure daughters
Of the gallant South
Who were weeping and screaming
In their dampened seats.

Episteme

In the end it all
boils down to
the difference in
knowing what "fishing"
means and knowing
where to fish—

Father's Day

Wherever my father was,
Children surrounded him.
Petitioning the Court of Time,
This is my final summation.

Fathers and Sons

Since that endless day
When my Father
Blew off half of his head
In the parking lot
Of a liquor store
Not far from the ocean
I have inhabited
A private wilderness.
I try to watch my step.

First Grade

On my first day of school,
at the door of my first classroom,
a black-haired girl came up
and kissed me violently.
I love you, she said.
Then she ran off down the hall.
I never saw her again,
and I never stopped looking.

Florentines

Cosi, tra questa Immensita s'annega il pensier mio:
E il naufragar m'e dolce in questo mare.

1

On the slow diretto
from Rome to Florence
your body breaks up slowly,
like a boat on the rocks,
and sleep is shallow.

Across the compartment
a man nods off, his head
lolls and juggles
on the crushed velvet
Under the framed

Amphetamine ad.
"Depression is a chain
Around your spirit,"
Says the ad,
As the train rolls on.

2

The smiling woman
With the high cheekbones
Shoves her fist
Into la puncinella

Trying to coax
An answer out of her
Wandering toddler son.
She stands him still.
He stares through her,
A fish staring through
The wavering bars
Of its water.

"And why has la puncinella come to visit?"

"Non lo so."

"And where have you been with your mama?

"Non lo so."

His shoulders hunch quickly—
Then he throws them back like wings—like wing stubs—
Trying to break
The strings he loves . . .

3

Ahead, on a hill
A broken tower rises
Out of the grey.
The pigeons and swallows
Rise, break flight, then
Disappear into its high
Angular coves of stone.
See how the stone comes
Alive as the birds enter it,
Much like memory.

4

The bar near the station
Is called The Recent Past.
When you open the door
You are stepping into
The last week or two,
having spent a lot of time in
The Recent Past of late,
and all your friends are there.

Here's Jimmy,
The "most deported man in Europe,"
despising the French
lustily, being Algerian.
"Once," he says, "I walk in a

bar in Marseilles, there's a
big sign up on the wall
that says "No Algerians
or dogs allowed! No Algerians
or dogs allowed, the
motherfuckers!"

Here's the Contessa,
an old woman with
brightly-colored bits
of broken glass wired
around her neck.
She sparkles like a car wreck,
listening to Jimmy,
singing to herself in French.

Here's the mad inventor,
tooling up in his anti-smog
mobile, shoving his lab coat
and his goggles under the dash,
pushing through the glass door,
his whole body a kind
of distracted nod, his
horn-rimmed glasses
low on his nose.
"Three important things
have been invented here
in Florence," he announces.
"The telephone, the atomic
reactor, and now . . . and now!"

You need to visit the bathroom badly,
but you can't go in there
without a strong sense
of impending loss. You enter anyway,
a veteran, and naturally
last week's news is nailed up
over the walls, and more is stuffed
into the stained ceramic niche
where the toilet paper should be.
You settle in for a long stay.
You will make it last.
The bar is called The Recent Past.

5

At a theatre near you: *Savannah Violenta!*
Piu impressionante del primo!
Across a plain five savages carry a dead man,
snakes snapping playfully at their heels.
They reach the desert,
they stake out a spot,
they build out of things at hand a low bier,
tumbleweeds woven together
and stretched across a square platform
built of bones. Big pommels of snakeskin
fitted to the legs to keep rats off.
The sky is empty. The sun
rolls on the rim of the earth.
They lay the dead man on the beir

and go away. Three days later
they return with an old Retsina bottle.
In the desert sun, the dead man
has risen like a well-made cake.
With a long, serrated knife
the savages cut his throat
And drain away the viscous white fluid
his blood has become.
They watch the sky; the sky is empty.
They will be leaders! In the last scene
we see that these are the men
our grandchildren become;
that these are our founding fathers!
In the last scene we realize
that nothing changes. In the last scene
huge mutant pigeons lift the fiats
off the piazzas, and they must have
rewound the godamned thing because

6

Ski troopers in cowboy boots
Comb the slopes at dawn.
The towns are unprepared for this.
Snowed-in gutters gurgle and hiss.
Dead birds litter the lawn.
Dead birds litter the lawn!

Massacio Rossi died today
With a bullet to the brain.
He was leaving the city to save his life
With his family and his future wife—
Everyone missed the train.
Everyone missed the train!

He was leaving the city to save his life;
He was tired of living there,
With the fascists tapping his telephone
And his mother afraid to live alone—
There was murder in the air.
There was murder in the air!

He packed a bag and grabbed his kin
And started out at night—
But the pistol caught him at the cab.
The killer's dress was described as "drab."
The others got out alright.
The others got out alright!

So tomorrow the demonstrations start—
The first is set for noon—
But the cops are getting nowhere fast,
Just as they have with assasins past—
It will be forgotten soon.
It will be forgotten soon!

7

"Behold the sword-tailed beast
That infects the world!
His just face— the body of a serpent!
His back and chest like spider webs.
He appears as if from the depths
Of a pool, then surfaces,
Then lies to like a boat at bay."

"Charon has eyes
Like wheels of fire
That light the way
Cross Acheron—"

"Laughing then, and tormenting souls
Afloat in the river of burning pitch,
A Demon called out over the wailing
'Did you not know Death is a logician?'"

8

Back in the barroom
the tables are empty,
the chairs turned up over the tabletops,
a boy shorter than the broom sniffles,
sweeping up broken glass
as an old woman in a wooly coat,
her hair in a net,

kneels in the blackening suds
scrubbing a stain on the tile.
Whatever it is will not come out.
Behind the stainless steel counter
the barrista grins, pulls his comb,
calls his lover on the telephone,
it is time to pay, time to go,
it was raining but now it isn't.
You fasten your scarf, and then
you are through the door into the dark
and the cold wind whipping down
from Fiesole that is worth
crying over. Behind you at
The Recent Past the steel grates slam,
are locked. A lost kid is wailing.
A portly whore hugs herself
in the alley, and all the stoplights
blink "advance with caution."

9

I pass the underground garage full of birdcages
I pass women who have learned to say "Rumplestiltskin"
   aloud, and emerge from the bedroom whole
I pass the all night *farmacia*
I pass under the benediction of the mannequins
I pass the murdered librarian who sleeps in the bank
I pass the sky in disguise
I pass the wiry short order cook who was jilted in 1951

I pass the legless beggar who seems to lose a limb a week
I check my arms, my legs, I walk faster
I pass and everything I pass I pass for the final time—
the last pissed-off sheriffs arrest one another in despair.

10

The bridge I am standing on
starts to buckle, or does it?
I throw my hat over the railing,
I kick my shoes off, I take
the rolled up newspaper
from under my arm
and tear it to shreds.
The ripped pieces turn to gulls
when I fling them into the wind.
The one history we share is madness.
I dance and fly, my arms full of air.
It is autumn all over the world.

Folie à Deux

Their eyes locked horns;
They married in haste.
Now they're divorced
And he's deceased—
An all too casual disgrace—
A tragedy, but commonplace.

Genie

Your command is my wish—
Though it wouldn't be so
If you weren't such a dish,
As I know that you know—

God

Everywhere
Nowhere
Somewhere
Way down there
Or up in the air
Anywhere
Elsewhere

Google is Eating Our Brains

In many instances
Wondering is better by far
than knowing for sure.

Gulls

Northeaster blowing—
grey, wet, cold and lovely—
gulls beating their way upstream
beside the boat
in slow motion—
their flinty eyes
fixed on the roiling water—

Halloween in Dothan

My dad would suspend
a ghostly, wraithlike
figure in a tree,
with a rope that ran
to our front door.
When kids came up to trick or treat,
he would wait till the perfect moment,
then drop the effigy in front of them,
with a loud, ghastly
horrorshow shriek!
Their cries of terror
and glee resound in
my haunted, uncertain memory
of Alabama 60 years on.

He Who Sings

He who sings
They say prays twice—
And sooner or later
He pays the price.

Helen's Wake

Swiftly the Greeks designed revenge—
The Trojans hid their plunder—
Far to sea a wave was formed
That swept both nations under.

History

Misremembering
on purpose
is what we call History.

Hitchhiker

Once I'd have stopped
For the tall indifferent stranger
In the floppy hat
With his thumb stuck out
Headed for nowhere—
Once I would have—
But by now my heart is hardened
Like old pine left underwater
For a hundred years
And I don't trust a soul.

Honour

Honour Is always
Spoken of
By those who never
Had their way.

Horse

The long, alien face of the horse
Said, "Yes—forever—
As long as you go there with me."

Interview

Many years ago I had a job interview
with a woman who was obviously
so distressed and distracted that
she barely knew where she was.
I needed the job, but we never got there—
she started to weep uncontrollably
and told me that her husband, a police detective
from whom she was divorcing,
had promised that he was going to kill her.
She knew he meant it. There was no way
to go to the police; he was the police.
She was, she said, waiting every day to die violently.
I did what I could to help her then,
in those strange conditions, but she was in shreds.
A few days on I read of her murder,
in the parking lot of a Publix, by her former husband,
the father of her children. I am to blame,
and everyone I know is guilty.
Some weeks later I was offered the job.

Intimacy

What could be
more intimate
than springing from a seed?

Italian Movie

In this gory Italian movie
you can tell the true psycho-killer
because he wears his mask to bed
Even when sleeping alone.

Jeremiad

Amused, I awaken
To ironically
Autobiographical
Jeremiads,
Aimed at others
But boomeranging,
Filled with rage
And resentment,
Utterly devoid
Of self-awareness,
Declaimed to mirrors
In the raw dawn.

Jingoism

Seeing through
all this jingoism
is the real human act.
Few have; few do;
few ever will.

Jukebox

Nothing like solitude,
a stiff drink,
and a great jukebox!

Kiss

There is no such thing
as a stolen kiss

Leave

There is no place to leave,
and no place to go.
There is only one place.

Life

A numbing series
Of irreversible losses
Ending in oblivion

Lion

There is a poem
That I think I wrote
As I slept in the tall, fragrant grasses.
I am still running it down
By light of dawn.

London

In the Tube in London
I looked up from a newspaper
to find a friend
from my hometown
looking up from his newspaper at me.
Then the train shuddered
and the lights went out.

Macbeth

Any demon can rule a man
By telling him what he wants to hear
Through the mouth of a woman
He's learned to fear,
Having loved her beyond his means.
All good witches adopt this plan.

Metaphors

Metaphors are the
Evasions we live by—
God is the first metaphor;
History the second.

Milky Way

Better than any mountaintop
From a darkened ship
A thousand miles at sea
I saw the fathomless depths
Surrounding the hub
Of the burning axis,
The tip of the burning wheel.

Mother

The world is never
Quite the same
Without your Mother in it.

My Style

Classical, in the early sense.
Ionic, not Corinthian.
No words wasted, but none withheld.
Pointed but guileless.
Built to last in the open air.

No Horizons

I was on a Destroyer,
smack in the middle
of the dark blue Atlantic.
We had a party on the steel deck
one cloudless afternoon—barbecue,
sound system—ship's band played—
then some fool spun
"The Wreck of the Edmund Fitzgerald,"
and every sailor grew silent,
and every sailor thought about home.
There were no horizons.

Numbers

I choke with utter exasperation
when people say,
with a knowing nod, sagely,
in irrefutable summation,
"Numbers don't lie."

Of course they do.
They always have. It depends
on whose numbers they are.
"Numbers" are not "math."
Numbers are somebody's math.

Orizon

(for my Father)

This Armistice Day
Let us first recall
The burned and mangled bodies
At bottom of it all
For whom we pray.

Orwell

Lie, then plainly lie again,
Then continue lying until
The lie is the truth
In the lied-to minds
Of those who sleep
Soundly, resting assured
Their leaders will never lie.
Then just keep lying.

Passage Hence

Stuck in the mindless
coming and going,
in a horrible haste
to get somewhere,
when the path itself
Is all worth knowing.

Patience Etude

On a glorious day,
much like today,
in the late afternoon,
find the last patch of sun.
Sit there. Think of nothing—
not even of the girl,
or the glass of whiskey.
Idly attend the sounds of the world.
Note, as though for the very first time,
that the leaves of the trees are translucent.
Remember, the more you forget the sun,
the faster it falls. Watch
the shade come on like a tide. Stay
till the shadows surround your head. Stay
till it's dark. Then simply stay.
Then go inside.

Penumbra

The headless man who shadows me
Can neither reason, smell, nor see—
He's a battered brainless homeless clone—
Slim as a snake, and all alone—
And yet, he seeks my sympathy!
He clings like a vine, his steps dog mine,
Like a husband tracking his wife online!

Permanent War

Permanent war:
A condition
of continued prosperity.

Poetry

An effulgence of mind
A brimming-over
of thought into
motile crystalline form
A spring with no source

Politics

I was sitting at a table
in a bar called the Pastime
when an agitated, saucer-eyed
kid came up to me, his fists clenched.
"I saw you looking at my girlfriend,"
he said. I looked around.
"Who's your girlfriend?"
He glared at me with opiate intensity,
raised up on his toes,
and said "Are you calling
my girlfriend a liar?" This is what
politics feels like today.

Predictive Intelligence

There are few things more galling
Than an ignorant headmaster.

Pryor

Like Nietzsche, the last thing you did
was stand up for an animal.
Right on, motherfucker!

Born unafraid— even of Dracula—
you picked up the bill and payed.
Right on, motherfucker!

As soon as I heard "That Nigger's Crazy"
I knew I'd been lazy.
Right on, motherfucker!

All night long, reaching for elsewhere,
winos raise glasses to the Man!
Right on, motherfucker!

Q

Engaged in sociopathic madness
modelled on video games,
pseudomythological quest sagas,
and scavenger hunts,
They wouldn't want
to compromise their alienation—
What's a conspiracy without it?

Rain

I love this kind of rain—
just as much
as the ground allows.

Rock and Roll

The rule in rock and roll is always:
Get the women dancing—
all the rest will follow.
And that's what is happening now—
The women are dancing.

Saudi

In the old cities,
they move through their daily duties
like wraiths, clad in black body veils—
only a fierce flash of the green eyes
to remind you
what women are.

Silence

We lost
the sister arts
of silence and stillness
long ago.

Silk

Silk, though sheer,
is strangely warm . . .

Song for Loodie

Our sweetest child LeeAnn is gone—
I never wanted to write this tune!
She lived more life than five girls could;
Maybe that's why she left so soon.
Cancel all flights tlll the party's over!
Dance to her by light of the moon!

SPQR

At last a long line of prisoners appeared,
Dust-covered, downfallen, doomed,
Paraded in chains between the war elephants,
Driven at last through the gate and into the long
Road to Rome, and Avernus.
This was the last time I saw my father.

Star

I think
I will love you
Even after I die,
When my vagrant atoms
Are spread across space,
There will be some
Flinty spark,
Hard as a diamond
And motile as fire:
Our star.

Sun and Moon

Each of us sees
the same sun and
the same moon.

Symposium

Louise, and Borges, and Eva Gabor
Were talking things over on the bedroom floor;
I took notes on the bathroom door
And all that was written disappeared with ease—
Eva said, "Darling, get me out of here please!"

Louise said, "This place has the languor of dreams."
Borges said, "Nothing is quite as it seems."
I did cartwheels in the ceiling beams,
Muttering post-modern melodies—
Eva said, "Darling, get me out of here please!"

This went on for a lifetime or more,
With the four of us locked in the plush boudoir,
Till somebody called for a company car
That arrived in the snow, in the shade of the trees—
Eva said, "Darling, get me out of here please!"

Thalassa

Poor
Sad
Poisoned
Mother
Ocean

Thanksgiving

The only safe way
To travel home
Is slowly, on foot,
on your own.

The Empire

Ah, they're off to war—
but look now, I'm damned
if they haven't paused
again to commemorate
the Queen's Own Annual Gala Celebration,
as they do every year,
wherever they are,
in blithe united oblivion.

The Gift

It is worse than a curse
But it hasn't killed me—
So I guess it's a gift
Some ancestor willed me.

The Last Part

You claim to be talking in tongues
But your words are weighted.
Each of them knows too well what it is
And settles on the page like a dollar bill
You are trying to save,
As every breeze blows you away.

The New Law

Told plain, the new law is,
if you have a bad feeling
about somebody's intent,
you can shoot them on the spot.
This is insanity, and opens wide
the gates to fascism.

The News

Mars has been Earth, Earth will be Mars—
This is the news from distant stars.

The Priest

Please pass
the collection plate—
Then, please,
pass it to me!

The Same

Yes, we are equal—
But we are not and cannot
Ever be the same.

The Thing

There's a thing
you felt, a thing you
knew very well as a child,
a thing they try very hard
to make you forget.

This is the thing
you can never
afford to forget.

Thinking

If you think at all—
And any time you are thinking—

You think with your whole body
And all your senses.

Three Wise Men

Where, this Christmas,
will I find three wise men?
Only at Lowes!

Time

Whatever it should do,
what it does do
is move faster the older we get
as our bodies are ever more
filled with of the past.

To a Trauma Junkie

Stop remembering—
But never forget.

To Creationists

"Must" and "God"
are not words
that go together well—
If He is all you say
He's all-powerful, you see,
and thus compelled to do
nothing whatsoever.

Underground Alien

I was taking the subway
back to Brooklyn after a show.
My guitar—68 Fender Jazzmaster,
hard shell case—
was against my knees.
There was no one else in the car.
Suddenly the rear doors
burst open and this dude
dressed like a pimp
came onto the empty stage.
He made a point of crossing me
and blundering against my shoe—
as he meant to.
Everything was unfolding
like a scene I had studied long ago.
He threatened to kill me
unless I paid his drycleaning bill.
I refused. In fact, I said
"I'm not paying for shit."
He said he had a gun
and was going to blow my brains out.
I said, go ahead. It was late.
He looked at me as though
I were from another planet
and said: "You a crazy motherfucker."
I nodded in agreement,
and he scuttled on up the train.

Velvet

As I click off the TV
Night in a cloak of velvet
Covering a pink kimono
Comes hither, softly.

Wood

I am become
Like an old root
Just above ground
All weathered
Without an idea
But wholly present
Feeding the tree

About the Author

Hal Steven Shows grew up in and around the beach towns of North Florida. He spent much of the 1970's living in Florence, Italy, where he worked as a waiter, a salesman of gold and silver, a teacher of English, and a translator. These years gave him the chance to explore Europe from Edinburgh to the Peloponnese. A graduate of the writing programs at Florida State University and Goddard College, he has translated the work of Cavalcanti, Leopardi, Rilke, Ungaretti, Pasolini, Gatto and others, and written extensively on literature and popular culture. Since the early 1980's he has been writing, performing, and recording music that defies genre but is actually only rock and roll. He lives near Tallahassee, Florida, where he owns and operates Witchingstick Studio.

Mr. Shows is a State of Florida Individual Artist Fellow and a member of the National Academy of Recording Arts and Sciences. A chapbook of his poems, *A Breath for Nothing*, appeared from the Anhinga Press in 1977. With the indie-rock band Persian Gulf he released *Changing the Weather* (1984), *Persian Gulf: The Movie* (1986), *Trailer* (1987), and *Cave Art Collective* (2001). Subsequent solo productions include *Birthday Suit* (1990), *Lifeboat* (1995), *Whitman's Sampler* (2000), *Native Dancer* (2003), and *Treasure of Love,* (2012). With the garage-rock ensemble Kangaroo Court, he has released the single "Grandaddy Yule" (1986), the album *Masque*, from the plague year 2021, and the EP *Holy Cats* in 2022. *Parasol*, a volume of poems, was published in 2007. *The Bandshell Project* (2015; 2nd edition 2016) is a collection of essays on music and poetry.

Acknowledgements

The author wishes to acknowledge those instrumental in bringing these *Chanterelles* to light. Without Carter Monroe's encouragement and help, this book would not exist. My musical comrades Mike Phillips and Mick Buchanan have helped me to focus my mind on writing what can be remembered. Jim Lōser has been invaluable in shaping the manuscript. And I wish to thank my teachers and mentors Van Brock, Michael Ryan, and Louise Glück, for their patience and wisdom. Last but first, thanks to Mara Landsman Shows for giving me a home where chanterelles can appear as they may.

www.ingramcontent.com/pod-product-compliance
Lightning Source LLC
Chambersburg PA
CBHW071230090426
42736CB00014B/3032